MY FALKLAND ISLANDS LIFE

-

ONE FAMILY'S
VERY BRITISH ADVENTURE

Jen Carter

Edited by Gillian Birch.

Front cover illustration by Mike Swallow.

My Falkland Islands Life - One Family's Very British Adventure
Jen Carter. -- 1st ed.
ISBN 978-1-908567-45-1

Contents

*Dedicated to the people of the Falkland Islands,
with grateful thanks for giving us such a warm welcome*

*Wilderness is not only a haven for native plants and animals
but it is also a refuge from society.*

*Its a place to go to hear the wind and little else,
see the stars and the galaxies.*

—JOHN MUIR

Introduction

In 1982, 8000 miles away from the UK, a bitter and bloody war was fought over the Falkland Islands.

But what is it about the Islands and their people that make them worth fighting for? Why is it that people who have visited the Islands, so often hanker to return to them?

Our family came to the Falklands unexpectedly, just after the end of the War.

We discovered a people and their way of life that we fell in love with. A people who are resilient, resourceful, hard-working and determined, with a real zest for life.

The Falkland Islands are a place time forgot. The Islanders are a tight-knit community, living a self-sufficient lifestyle that most can only dream of.

This book is my attempt to pull the wraps off the Islands, to show the heart and passion of the Islanders themselves and to take a look behind the scenes at their very British way of life.

My hope is that you will hear something of the beating heart of the Islands, the heart that beats behind the beauty and wildlife that draw you to the Falklands.

You'll see some of the ups and downs of living a self-sufficient lifestyle in such a remote location, far away from the hustle and bustle of city life.

Finally, I hope you may discover something of what makes this people and this place worth fighting for.

<u>CHAPTER 1</u>

Our Story

As seasoned travellers, Andrew and I could never have dreamt of the adventure that was just around the corner.

For the previous two years, my husband had been studying for an MSc (Master of Science) in Tropical Agriculture with the University of Reading. He spent the first year living and studying at the university, followed by another year living in Port Harcourt, Nigeria, learning his trade as an agronomist.

Andrew's study and travel, was funded by the then Overseas Development Administration's (ODA), a branch of the government whose role was to encourage and train up those in so-called developing countries. When Andrew's class graduated, there were few job opportunities for expensively trained agronomists. This seemed illogical in the extreme, since thousands of pounds had been invested in each student.

Skeptically, I sometimes wondered whether part of the reason for the entire program was so that someone could answer a question in the House of Commons on how much the UK was investing financially in the support of agriculture in developing countries.

So, at the end of two years of hard work and study, there were no job opportunities overseas for my husband. As luck would have it, one of his tutors saw his potential and offered him a short-term post working at the ODA headquarters in London.

Andrew and Jennifer with newborn baby, Martin

After a few months of long hours, commuting daily from Bournemouth to London, we were both desperate for a more manageable lifestyle.

It was at this point, one of his colleagues made a somewhat unexpected suggestion, particularly to someone who specialised in Tropical Agriculture.

"There's an opening for an agronomist in the Falkland Islands", his colleague began, "and I think it would suit you and your family right down to the ground!".

"Where?"

It was 1986 and despite the Falklands War having only recently ended, I needed to get out our Times Atlas to find out exactly where the Islands were located. The Islands themselves are east of Argentina, with nothing but ocean separating them from the frozen landscape of Antarctica.

And so it came about that we sat down as a couple to discuss the idea of moving as a family to the Falkland Islands. Andrew's colleague himself had already visited the Falkland Islands, knew much about the lifestyle there and was able to tell us about what we might expect.

As we began to grasp more of what the role would involve, we also began to uncover more about the lifestyle that we would be adopting. Our transition would be from the bustling city of Bournemouth in the south of England to a small community in West Falkland, surrounded by wide-open spaces and living a self-sufficient lifestyle out of necessity rather than choice.

One of the most well-thumbed books on our bookshelf was John Seymour's book, Self-Sufficiency. For two keen but clueless enthusiasts, the opportunity to "live the good life" sounded almost too good to be true.

Living in such a far-flung place as the Falkland Islands, the biggest challenge we felt at the time, was the distance between ourselves and our families, as our son Martin was only a few months old. To be honest, there was never really a choice. This was an adventure we simply couldn't turn down.

Though we had hankered after a posting in warmer climes, as we'd experienced in Africa, the Falkland Islands were already starting to find a place in our hearts.

Martin with Tristar behind

And so, after a few intense weeks of preparation, we found ourselves at Brize Norton in Oxfordshire waiting to board a Tristar flight to the Falkland Islands.

We were off on the adventure of a lifetime!

CHAPTER 2

The Falkland Islands & Fox Bay

The flight to the Falkland Islands took nearly 20 hours, covering a 7,858-mile journey. Several of the seats on the Tristar aircraft were empty, leaving plenty of room for us to stretch out, move around and keep our five-month-old son entertained.

We enjoyed stretching our legs during a short break for refuelling at Ascension Island. Baby Martin was memorably fast asleep at the delightfully named Wide Awake Airport. Balmy temperatures provided a pleasant place for us to stretch our legs before re-boarding the plane.

Just to put you in the picture, the Falkland Islands are somewhat larger than most people think, being made up of over 700 islands and covering an area about the size of Wales.

There are two main islands, East Falkland and West Falkland, with more than half the population living in the capital, Port Stanley, known as Stanley to the islanders.

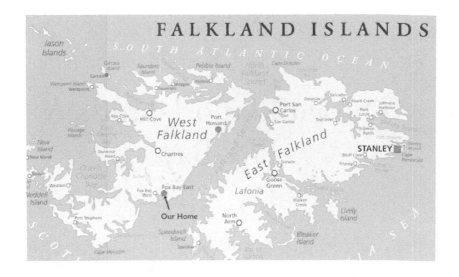

Map of the Falkland Islands,
with Fox Bay and Stanley marked

Beyond Stanley, there are a number of farms and settlements where the remainder of the population live. This is known locally as 'Camp'.

At latitude 51°S, Stanley is situated roughly as far south of the equator as London is to the north. It comes as a surprise to many to learn that Stanley has more sunshine hours in a year than Kew Gardens.

Whilst the climate in the Falklands is somewhat similar to the UK, the winds are generally more frequent and stronger, and the temperature range is narrower. The wind is also colder, blowing straight from the Antarctic. The temperature rarely gets above 20° centigrade, but can feel warmer. On the plus side, frost is infrequent and snow never hangs around for long.

Fox Bay, where we lived, is one of the largest of around eight settlements on West Falkland, and is situated on the east coast.

Substantial government funding has been invested to develop Fox Bay as a 'centre of development' on the west island. There are two settlements at Fox Bay: Fox Bay West and Fox Bay East, which became known as Fox Bay Village during our time in the islands.

Fox Bay Village from the air
(taken in 2015 by Terry Mooney, Winch Operator)

Fox Bay Village comprised of a dozen houses and families; in total about 40 individuals. Along with a Post Office, the Salmon Project and the Falkland Islands Mill, the village was home to some mill workers, two independent contractors, two Packe section farmers, ourselves and another agricultural researchworker, together with their families. There was also a detachment of soldiers based at nearby Shag Cove for army adventure training, with a number of RAF refuellers staying at the Bunkhouse.

When we arrived, we quickly realised that the recent Falklands War had clearly left its marks on those who had lived through it in Fox Bay. It was not just the landscape and the buildings which told the tale of what had happened, nor the fenced-off minefields that surrounded the village and the school building with the Red Cross painted on the roof. What happened in those 74 intense days had left its indelible mark on every single person.

Andrew and Martin meet the penguins!

Imagine, if you will, a small British village, with a slow pace of life, where the seasons come and go and life is simple and predictable.

Into this, unexpected and uninvited, come Argentinian soldiers, with the dubious mission of what they believed to be reclaiming Argentinian soil. Imagine their surprise when confronted with a very British way of life and fierce resistance from the locals.

Everything changed during the invasion. Thousands of Argentine troops were placed on the islands - guards were placed outside individuals' homes, asking them where they were going and what they were doing. Many Islanders stayed in their homes, keen to hold things together, though some of the more outspoken locals were arrested and thrown out, repatriated to the UK for the duration of the war.

During our time in the Falklands, I do not believe I heard one single redeeming story about the Argentine soldiers. On the few occasions when people chose to look back and remember those terrible days, there were warm stories about the liberation, fond memories of the men and women who liberated them, friendships built, and the joy of freedom when all had seemed lost.

*Andrew, with Martin on his shoulders
and Devon & Dorset soldiers in front*

Our own arrival in Fox Bay coincided with a time of huge change, partly precipitated by the recent conflict. Packe Brothers, who had run massive farms across the Islands, were being broken down into smaller, family-owned and run farms.

As we arrived, individuals were transitioning from working for a large organisation, to owning and working their own land. During our time there, Fox Bay West, just across the water, was split into six 'small' sections over a couple of seasons. These smaller sections were not just a few acres; the packages of farmland often incorporated thousands of acres.

Sand Pond Stream, near Fox Bay

For these men and women, this really was the 'new frontier' - a modern day "Gold Rush"; an opportunity like no other. These were true pioneers, willing to risk everything for the privilege of calling this patch of land their own. This was no easy ride, but rather a commitment to a life of hard graft and isolation, in return for the privilege of owning your own piece of the Falklands.

Following the war, the Shackleton Report prompted the setting up of the Falkland Islands Development Corporation (FIDC), funded by a multi-million pound investment package from the UK government.

The aim was to facilitate a number of start-up businesses, broadening the income base of the islanders, thus ensuring they were less dependent on the sale of wool in order to secure their financial future. As a result of this investment, a number of new ventures were launched in Fox Bay, including the Falkland Islands Mill and the Salmon Farm.

It was as part of this raft of funding that we ourselves arrived in the Falklands with the mission to explore and develop the potential for the vast grasslands of the islands including tussac grass, which grows naturally in some areas of the Falklands.

View across Fox Bay

Everyone I have met who has visited the Falkland Islands, has been captivated by the people and the way of life. The Islands and their people quickly find a place in people's hearts, they're somewhere visitors dream of and hanker to return to.

CHAPTER 3

First Impressions
of Port Stanley

Somewhat bleary eyed, we arrived at the newly-built Mount Pleasant Airport at Port Stanley and were immediately ushered into a large hanger, directed to hard seats, and given a long safety briefing.

This eye-opening briefing included how to spot mined areas, where to avoid, what to look out for and what to do if you spotted anything suspicious. It was accompanied by images of what might occur if you ignored these warnings. What a sobering welcome to the Falkland Islands!

Mount Pleasant Airport (MPA) from the air

As we stepped out of the airport, an array of vehicles, mainly Land Rovers, greeted the arriving passengers. At that time, the Land Rover was ubiquitous in the Falkland Islands. The Land Rover was pretty much the only vehicle which was capable of coping with the rough terrain, was reliable and easy to maintain. Loading our suitcases into the back of a Land Rover, we were driven along the long gravel road to Port Stanley at a fair lick.

Martin & Andrew, with the 110 Landrover
we used for journeys across Camp on West Falkland

It is 37 miles from the airport to Stanley and even at a good speed it took over an hour. Only later did we learn that this was one of the best roads in the whole of the islands. It had recently been built to accommodate the increasing amount of traffic between Mount Pleasant Airport (MPA), the forces base, and Port Stanley itself. The roads in Port Stanley were of a good standard, but once you left the town they were mainly rough tracks; nothing you could reasonably describe as a road.

Our accommodation in Stanley for the first few days was at a pretty little bed and breakfast, or B&B, called Emma's Guest House in a 1930s-style terrace. Close to the jetty, it overlooked the water where ships and stores frequently arrived from the UK.

Emma's Guest House was just around the corner from West Store, which had a comprehensive range of just about everything any self-respecting Falkland Island resident could ever need.

Port Stanley, as viewed from
the FIGAS Islander aircraft

Our first few days passed quickly as my husband Andrew was briefed for his new job at the Agricultural Research Centre in Port Stanley and got to know the small team. For me, it was the perfect opportunity to explore the island's capital and meet some of its thousand-or-more inhabitants.

The sizeable box containing our belongings,
shipped by sea from the UK

Another reason for our time in Stanley was waiting for the arrival of our goods from the UK, which came by ship. Once the shipping container arrived in Stanley, it was transferred to the MV Forrest, a small fisheries research vessel, and shipped to Fox Bay, where we were to spend the next two years of our life.

Development since the 1982 conflict was evident on our arrival, only four years later. There was a new hospital and 'Brewster' kit houses were being constructed to accommodate the increasing population, many of whom were arriving as part of a package to develop and rebuild the Falklands.

The new Scandinavian-style homes were in striking contrast to the original houses. They were timber-framed, triple-glazed buildings full of every modern feature and were a world apart from the corrugated roofs and colourfully painted single-glazed homes that typify Falkland Island architecture, both in Stanley and beyond.

One of the new 'Brewster' houses in Stanley

Stanley, the tiny capital of the Falkland Islands, was a capital like no other. People greet you in the street, acknowledge you when you stop to let them across a zebra crossing and are happy to talk to you in the shop. No-one is in too much of a rush to acknowledge you.

My first impressions of Port Stanley include the fabulous colours of the buildings, the deep red of the Falkland Islands store, the beautiful whalebone arch by the church, the walk along the shore up to Government House and the old wreck of the Lady Elizabeth marooned in the channel nearby.

*Jen, with baby Alissa under her Fjällräven jacket (yes, really!),
and Martin in the stroller on a chilly day in Port Stanley*

I remember visiting three shops in Stanley. One was full of tourist items such as cute stuffed toy penguins and postcards, original paintings and prints by local artists. The second, further north and near the hospital if I remember rightly, was a small store crammed with canned goods and other essential items.

The crowning glory of all the Stanley shops was West Store, where anything and everything could be purchased. It was the equivalent of a modern hypermarket, yet much smaller, stocking everything from sunglasses, wellies and ATV parts to tins of mandarin oranges, swimming costumes and meat saws.

A traditional home in the Islands

West Store was also the only place on the island where you could buy some of these key essential goods, unless you ordered them in from the UK, which could otherwise take months. West Store was a veritable emporium of delights, a place to spend hours exploring and discovering things you never knew you needed.

We made the most of our time in Stanley, getting to know our way around and knowing our stay wouldn't last for long. This was only a stopover before reaching our final destination, our new home in Fox Bay.

CHAPTER 4

Our New Home in Fox Bay

Excitement grew as we prepared to fly out to our new home on West Falkland.

Austin, Andrew's new colleague, and his wife Angela, had been kind enough to send us a comprehensive letter covering what to expect on our arrival. They included a sketch map of Fox Bay, giving us an idea of the scale of the settlement.

The homes of about 10 families were marked on the settlement, showing our house in the "city centre", right on the main track. There was also a military camp close to Fox Bay with around 100 servicemen, although this was phased out during our time there.

We'd also been given a booklet from Andrew's employer, "Falkland Islands - Notes on living conditions for ODA sponsored personnel" which gave some useful information about living in the Islands, including:

"The ideal expatriate would be something of a paragon - stable, self-sufficient, easy-going and a good mixer, good host and cook, a determined optimist not to be put off by wind, snow, sleet, rain

or cold, with a do-it-yourself disposition and an irrepressible sense of humour, fond of open spaces, nature and gardening ... but many ordinary mortals with the good sense to accept the place as it is and to make the most of what it offers have been, and are, happy here."

This was some tall order for the perfect expatriate, and left us under no illusions of the challenges that might lay ahead.

Views across West Falkland, with snow on far hills

Another point which provided us with some amusement was:

"Tipping .. is not customary. Indeed, very few of the services for which tipping is customary ... are available here."

The booklet gave brief information about the general cost of living, suggesting that it would be "between two and three times the price you would expect to pay in a British supermarket, but local meat and fish are very much cheaper."

Prices were listed for local goods in Stanley, as at September 1984:

- Instant Coffee (200g) - £3.19
- Cornflakes (375g) - £1.12
- Orange marmalade (340g) - 60p
- Tinned tomatoes (396g) - 46p
- Stock cubes (12) - 66p
- Box of French red wine (3 litres) - £5.46
- Kenwood Chef - £102.36

Despite these helpful tips, we still had no real idea of what to expect on our arrival, but we did not have to wait long. The time soon came for us to take our first flight across to West Falkland and see Fox Bay for the first time.

The red and blue colours of the Islander aircraft,
as it prepares for takeoff

We travelled, as every Falkland Islander does, by Islander aircraft. Each plane was painted in an bright shade of red with a blue stripe along each side. The flight itinerary for each day was flexible, governed by who wanted to fly and where they needed to go. There was no such thing as a scheduled flight; you simply got in touch and told them where and when you want to fly, then the schedule for each day was put together.

Stanley airport was just a few minutes' drive from where we were staying. It was with great excitement that we climbed aboard the little plane for the journey to our new home. Flying over the Camp area, it was strikingly clear that this was a wild and barren land, with hardly any signs of human habitation.

West Head, Fox Bay Mountain & Kelp Point, at Fox Bay

Along the coastline we flew over gorgeous sandy beaches and a brilliant blue sea, which would not have looked out of place in the Caribbean. Inland, there were vast acres of uninhabited grasslands grazed by the occasional sheep. Our bird's eye view from the Islander was simply breathtaking.

The breaking waves of the South Atlantic

I do not know who was more excited - ourselves arriving at the settlement, or the islanders in Fox Bay where the "jungle drums" would have been communicating our arrival for several weeks before the event. For us, this move was so much more than just a job - it was an exciting adventure into the unknown. For the Islanders, we were new people to meet, get to know and share a rum toddy with.

As we came in to land, we could barely see the small landing strip, but the pilot dropped the plane down with an expert touch. In the coming months, we came to appreciate the great skill of the pilots in landing an Islander aircraft in all weathers on such short airstrips, often with a fierce crosswind.

The main track through Fox Bay

We had thought that Fox Bay would be a fairly deserted spot, but as we surveyed our new village home, we were not fully prepared for how beautiful it was in its simplicity.

Bumping down the track in the Land Rover, we eagerly devoured our new surroundings – cream-painted houses with pretty red roofs, the small school building with a red cross on the roof and the incredible peace and quiet of our surroundings.

With a mixture of excitement and some trepidation, we were welcomed to our new home - a one storey building with a converted attic and a cheery yellow kitchen. Although somewhat in need of decoration, we loved it at first sight. At the heart of the house was a peat-fired Rayburn with a neat stack of peat outside to keep us cosy and warm in the coming winter.

Our new home in Fox Bay

It soon became apparent we had much to learn, not least how to keep the fire going in the Rayburn, how to use the new radio system to keep in touch, and how to grow our own vegetables, if we were to have them fresh.

As we settled down for the first night as a family in our new home, it was with smiles on our faces and a sense of expectation and anticipation. Our adventure was only just beginning.

CHAPTER 5

Life in Fox Bay

Our new home, situated on a windswept peninsular, was in astonishingly beautiful surroundings. We threw ourselves into settling into our home, learning the tasks and skills we needed in our new life.

We heard the somewhat unusual story of why our house was now empty. The previous owner, George Stewart, had been found dead on the kitchen floor, apparently having fallen and knocked his head on the Rayburn. We were sorry to hear of poor George's untimely end, but were very thankful to have our own little house, which we set about making into a home.

We were loaned some furniture, while we waited for our own shipment of belongings and furniture to arrive. It took us moments to fall in love with this little house, its cheerful yellow walls, patterned lino flooring and laminate-topped kitchen table.

It wasn't anything special, but to us it quickly became a place we could call home.

Initiation into Camp Life

Our home came with its own peat stack, with sufficient peat remaining to keep us warm until the next peat-cutting season. The peat-fired Rayburn did more than just heat our home; it was also our cooker and heated all our water via the back boiler.

The Rayburn was the heart of our home and a great place to lean against and warm yourself on a cold day.

The heart of our home - the Rayburn (with drying rack above)

We were quickly initiated into the mysteries of the RT, or RadioTelephone. This method of communication was as essential as our mobile phones are to us today.

The RT was a system of two-metre CB radios which were used to communicate both in the safety of the village and when travelling between settlements, across the wilder area of Camp.

As we were newcomers, everyone was keen to meet us. Whether they stopped to have a chat as we crossed the village green, or popped over and knocked on our door, the welcome was warm and friendly. No simple handshakes, or formal hellos, but, without exception, they would take their time to discover our story and share a little of theirs.

In our modern age of busy-ness, where people seem to always be rushing, Falkland Islanders always had time for other people. They were never waiting for life to happen, never too busy for the important things in life. If anyone could be said to be living in the moment and enjoying the present, it was the Islanders.

We had been advised to bring a radio with us, so we were soon initiated into the friendly sound of FIBS (Falkland Islands Broadcasting Station).

We soon got to know the delightful voice of Patrick Watts, who seemed to be on air every day, bringing updates and sharing community news.

FIBS radio helped to bring us closer and helped us to feel like we belonged to a wider community, even though everyone was spread out over a vast area of Camp.

Learning to fend for ourselves

In Camp, there was no regular supply of fresh fruit and vegetables. We soon realised that if we wanted to eat them, we had to grow them ourselves. With the salt-filled winds blowing straight off the South Atlantic and coming from the South Pole, a polytunnel was the only way to reliably grow your own food.

A few weeks after placing an order, our polytunnel duly arrived and we were ready to get started.

The' spot for fishing the Sand Pond Stream - 'Su's Hole'

The creativity of the green-fingered Falkland Islanders never ceased to amaze me. The most astonishing example was that of Shirley and Nigel, sheep farmers and landowners, who lived opposite us.

Shirley grew the most astonishing tomatoes I have ever seen. If anyone had green fingers, it was Shirley. I think she was probably helped a little by the fact that her raised beds included copious quantities of sheep manure collected from the shearing sheds, providing rocket fuel to her tall, leafy and prolific tomato plants.

Falkland Islanders excel in generosity, particularly with their time. When we needed to turn an area of hard ground behind our home into a potato plot, there was someone willing to harness up the rotovator and plough it up for us, turning a potentially back-breaking task into an enjoyable occasion.

Getting the ground ready for our polytunnel

Erecting our polytunnel was another community affair, similar to the barn raising one hears of back in the 18th and

19th centuries. It was a team event, placing the metal bars and pulling the heavy polytunnel cover into place.

As "green" novices, we found there was a definite art to creating a windproof door for entering the tunnel, which our neighbours kindly assisted us with. Last, but not least, it was essential to put the anti hotspot tape in just the right place, to prevent the incessant winds from ripping the tunnel.

The polytunnel is finally up!

Once our polytunnel was up, we got on with the task of growing our own vegetables, thanks to a wide array of Thomson and Morgan seeds. One of my guilty pleasures was to sit with the seed catalogue, dreaming and planning of what might be possible.

With planning and effort, we were able to grow courgettes, beans, peas, sweetcorn, Chinese cabbage, cucumbers, marrow and strawberries in this sheltered microcosm.

On grey days, the polytunnel was a warm and welcoming place to go, pulling in the warmth of the sunshine and shutting out the inclement weather.

Our young son Martin loved coming out to the polytunnel, his little feet picking the way between the plants. One of his favourite tricks was snapping off fresh pea pods and munching them.

Jen inside the polytunnel

In the warmth of the tunnel, the courgettes and beans really took off, allowing us to use the excess to make a delicious courgette chutney according to neighbour Carol's recipe. Other recipes shared with us indicate the types of excess that were typical in the Islands, such as spiced tomato relish, piccalilli, green tomato chutney and mustard sweet pickle.

To provide variety, we were occasionally able to order fresh vegetables from the newly-established hydroponics market garden in Stanley. This provided not only much-needed fresh vegetables, but also some amusement, as some of these vegetables were clearly new to the locals.

On one occasion we received a box of vegetables with an intriguing name listed on our shopping list - a "robshine". It took us several minutes to work out that the vegetable this was referring to was actually an aubergine. We still call aubergines "robshines" to this day!

Andrew with young Martin,
posing for a photo in the Landrover

Camp is a place of real community. Whatever anyone had in abundance, they were always happy to share. We never went short of vegetables in our first few weeks, as neighbours were happy to share theirs.

Martin enjoying an apple

This unstinting generosity applied across the board. If someone had a good catch of fish, had recently slaughtered an animal, or received a "goodie box" from visiting members of the forces, these were shared with friends, knowing the favour would be returned when someone else had excess themselves. One of these goodie boxes included some fresh fruit and it was such a joy to watch our young sons delight as he bit into his first orange.

Sharing was a simple enough idea, which drew us closer together as a community.

Our frontier lifestyle

As we settled into our new life, we began to learn some of the skills that were needed in our home. The most important one was not only to get a fire started in the Rayburn, but to keep it in overnight.

Young Martin looks on as his father, Andrew,
cuts peat from our peat bank

This involved the nightly selection of a 'banker', a chunk of peat of sufficient size and density that, by turning the Rayburn down low, you could keep the fire smouldering all night long, preventing the somewhat challenging and time-consuming task of restarting it in the morning.

There was a lot of manly joking about this. On the Falklands, it would seem that the quality of a man was not judged so much by his muscles, but by his ability to keep the fire in overnight!

After a few failures, we got the hang of this and enjoyed the wonderful smell of burning peat permeating our home.

Aerial view of the peat banks, where peat is cut each year

The next thing to get to grips with was our twin-tub washing machine, shipped out from Stanley. There was a whole new skill set to learn, having to wash the least dirty items first and then spin them, followed by the next most dirty items and finally the dark items, followed by the nappies. Every week, it took a full morning to do the washing.

Throughout our time in the Islands, we used terry cloth nappies for Martin, washing and drying them ourselves. What would today's mothers, who have disposable nappies so ready to hand, have thought?

A standard item in every Falkland Islands home was a drying rack. It hung above the Rayburn and was able to be raised and lowered, making it easy to hang and dry washing in the warmest place in the house, whatever the weather.

Loving our new self-sufficient family life in West Falkland

Another challenge was the art of hanging clothes on the washing line - not as straight forward as it might at first appear. On a calm day this was an easy affair, however, one never knew when a stiff breeze might blow up. We quickly learnt to close each peg firmly, in order to avoid the ignominy of having one's clothes blowing across the village green in full sight of the neighbours.

The trick was to use wooden pegs, rather than plastic ones, and to use double pegs for anything which might have a tendency to go walkabout in the wind, such as sheets, towels or nappies which created a natural 'sail' that caught the wind.

Even with all these precautions, on a couple of occasions we had to go hunting for items of clothing that had gone missing from our washing line, but were found nearby.

View of our neighbour's house

When we wanted to buy meat, we could not just go down to the local supermarket and buy it in neat packages, all ready to eat.

Instead, we had our own meat shed and Andrew had to master the art of butchery. Sheep are ubiquitous to the Falkland Islands, so our main meat source was sheep - not lamb, but mutton.

Sheep reared on the fine grasses of the Falkland Islands not only grow high quality wool, but amazingly tasty meat, with a deep rich flavour. Unlike some people's expectations, Falklands mutton was never dry and chewy but always mouthwateringly delicious and full of flavour.

West Heads from Kelp Point, Fox Bay

Animals were slaughtered by local farmers, and distribut-
ed in halves or quarters and left to hang in the meat shed to
mature. A freshly dressed mutton carcass cost around £8-£10
while a quarter of beef cost between £25 and £30, but was
only available in the winter.

Once the meat was delivered, there was no butcher to neatly
cut it up for you; it was your job to do the butchering yourself.
This was usually done on the kitchen table, which had a wipe
clean top for obvious reasons. Thankfully, for Andrew's first
time of butchering, our neighbour John was kind enough to talk
him through the process. After that, we were on our own.

Every Falkland Islander had one or more large deep
freezers in which to store meat, fish and frozen vegetables. The
seasonality of goods is very evident in the Islands, as it was not
possible to simply import or buy foods out of season.

Our large freezer became an essential part of our survival toolkit, as did managing our frozen supplies, saving particular joints for special occasions.

Fishing for our supper

An occasional treat was to eat gosling. Goose, being too tough, was mostly fed to the animals. To get a goose, one first needed to spot an upland goose, shoot and prepare it.

Andrew became a dab hand with the .22 rifle, spotting geese feeding on the short grass where the sheep were brought in before shearing, taking aim and firing. There is something genuinely satisfying about shooting, when you bring it home as food, whether for yourself or your animals.

Eggs were a challenge in our first few weeks. You only realise how essential eggs are to the home when you have to go without them for several weeks!

Every family had their own chickens and chicken run, which provided the eggs they needed for the family. They were fed on layers meal brought in large sacks from Stanley, together with the scraps from our kitchen table.

Fortunately for the chickens, the last warrah, or Falkland Island fox, had died out long ago so there were no predators for them, or indeed us, to worry about.

Eggs - our own pullet and hen's eggs,
compared to the size of a Mollymawk egg

Although Army eggs were occasionally available from visitors, it was essential to have your own supply. The contrast between army eggs and home-produced eggs was demonstrated in the lovely welcome cake that Shirley Knight made for us.

One layer of the sponge was a deep golden yellow, made from eggs from her own hens; the other layer was a more insipid colour, made from the battery hen eggs of the army. A real contrast!

We had inherited a chicken run that came with our house, just a short walk across the central green. In the same way that they are generous with other things, our neighbours were generous enough to furnish us with a couple of chickens. A few pullets were ordered from Stanley, though they took some months to mature and start laying eggs of any useful size.

Our first pullets, which took a while to lay us any eggs

This initial lack of eggs meant getting quite creative in the cooking line. It was several months before we really had enough eggs to not be really careful with our supply, so we learnt how to make eggless cakes until our own eggs came in. Our neighbours shared their own eggless recipes with us so that we could continue to enjoy cakes until we had our own egg supply.

We quickly realised that hens are seasonal layers. Their peak laying season is during summer, but although they will continue eating during the winter months, they cease laying any eggs.

This is a problem, as to make cakes and all manner of delicious things, one needs a year-round supply of eggs.

Our hen run, with rooster nicknamed 'Tunde' in charge

In our modern age, we take a plentiful supply of eggs for granted. The solution to this problem, was a marvellous compoundcalled water glass. Added to a large bucket of water in the appropriate quantities, you could place and preserve eggs in here, sealing and keeping them fresh for months, until required.

In an effort to provide more variety of meat during our time on the islands, we kept both pigs and ducks with mixed results.

We received the ducks as fertilised eggs which we kept in an incubator until they hatched out. For some reason, they didn't seem to thrive, even though we did our best to feed and keep them healthy.

Pigs, however, were another matter. Flown in by the FIGAS plane as piglets, the pigs were jointly shared between us and the

Birmingham's and they were a great success. The piglets were kept in a little run between our houses, with John and Andrew fencing this off using repurposed pallets.

The pigs were fed on left-over food from our homes, as well as excess milk from the dairy and any geese Andrew was able to shoot. As a result, the piglets grew quickly and we looked forward to the day when we could enjoy our own home-produced pork.

One of our pigs, in their run made from old pallets

The biggest challenge with the pigs arose on the day that they were due to be slaughtered. We had advised everyone in the village to keep clear of the area, as Andrew and John despatched them.

There was just one person who we had unfortunately not been able to get in touch with, and that was Jennifer, the only vegetarian in the village. We could hardly believe the appalling timing, as Jennifer happened to walk by our home just at the moment the pigs were being dispatched.

It could not have been worse. Jennifer, a relative newcomer to the islands, was horrified at the idea of killing an animal and was definitely not happy to have witnessed part of it. It was the subject of some discussion for days to come that, despite our best efforts to warn everyone in the village, the person who found it most distasteful was in fact the only person to have seen it.

Bread-making was another new skill to be learned. With no local bakery, the only option was to make it yourself. Thankfully, we had brought our own reliable Kenwood Chef with us. All that was required was to order a dough hook and we were in business with our own bread-making. The average Falkland Islanders eat a lot of bread, so flour was ordered in vast 50kg sacks and stored in a vermin-proof box. Ours was just the other side of the laundry room, adjacent to our freezer.

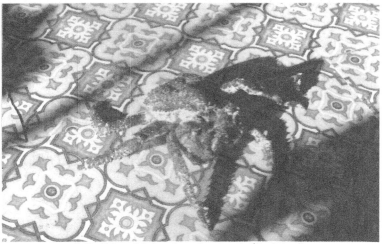

A Falkland Island crab on our kitchen floor -
the vessel researching this resource was based in Fox Bay

It took some time for me to get the hang of making bread, and more than a few disasters of glutinous, heavy and inedible results. I pummelled the dough until my wrists ached, but once the Kenwood dough hook arrived, I was able to consistently turn out tasty, well-risen bread.

With a little time and persistence, I felt that I could make bread with the best of them. There is nothing quite like the smell and taste of warm homemade bread, fresh from the oven, slathered with local butter and a dollop of jam!

Other seasonal delights included Christmas lamb, goslings, sea trout, mussels, squid and delicious freshly-picked tea berries. They tasted all the better, because they were fresh and all from our local area.

Our lifeline to Stanley, the FIGAS aircraft

An enjoyable new ritual was the post. Half an hour after the arrival of the FIGAS plane, which came most weekdays, postmaster Ken would be sorting the post, surrounded by a handful of folk eager to receive the latest news from family and friends.

Letters could take two to three weeks to arrive from the UK, but took a lot longer in the busy period leading up to Christmas. Sending letters, particularly birthday or Christmas cards, required quite some forethought. One had to source both the card and the gift, purchase or locate some suitable wrapping paper, then parcel them up and send them off in plenty of time to arrive safely in the UK.

Port Howard, a typical settlement on West Falkland

Writing letters was something of a time-consuming process, as we had to write them by hand or type them out on a typewriter, making corrections as we went along.

Letters were a lifeline to our family back home and receiving a letter was always a special time, as we sat and read the letter together.

The Fox Bay Post Office is quite well-known with philatelists, as the Fox Bay stamp on your mail is pretty unusual.

Andrew writes a letter home on our typewriter,
with Martin 'helping' out

Certainly the location of the Falkland Islands seems to have mystified more than one Royal Mail employee. At least one lot of post arrived stamped as having come via Bokoro, Papua New Guinea and Sydney, Australia before finally making its way to our little corner of the world in Fox Bay. It seemed that despite the recent war, the location of the Falkland Islands was still a mystery to some.

Electricity for the settlement was provided by a central generator, with power only available between six in the morning and midnight. It took some adjustment to adapt to this with a young child, as we often had to get up in the night. We soon got used to having a candle and matches by our bedside, and managed perfectly well during the hours of darkness.

Keeping healthy in a remote community

Looking back now, it seems a little terrifying that both myself and our neighbour Sue became pregnant and spent the first few months of our pregnancies so far away from immediate medical help. If this scared my mother, a trained nurse and midwife, she never let on about all the problems we could have faced. I gave birth back in the UK, whilst we were on leave, whilst Sue's baby was born in the Stanley hospital.

Fox Bay had regular visits from medical professionals who provided an opportunity for in-person diagnosis, vaccinations and so on. However, the majority of medical needs were dealt with over the communal phone at the Halliday's home. There was little privacy and no chance of sharing your illnesses and most private details with the doctor in person. Instead, you shared details with a faceless person on the end of a phone, unsure who else may be overhearing your conversation.

Beautiful Falkland skies

In such a close-knit community, nothing much seemed to stay private for very long. As you waited for your turn on the radio, there was more than a little speculation as to what the reason might be. This was the reality of sharing our lives as a community, we shared both the highs and the lows, few things were kept secret.

Despite this, medical support was of the highest quality. Any serious concerns saw you swiftly flown by FIGAS aeroplane into Stanley Hospital for further diagnosis or treatment. Memorable crises included our young son Martin suffering from diarrhoea and vomiting. On another occasion, Austin and Angela's young daughter Jessica had a bead stuck up her nose. Both incidents necessitated trips into Stanley. One Christmas, on returning from school, Shirley's boys brought a special gift with them - mumps!

Thankfully, we managed to survive all these mini-crises to continue enjoying life in Fox Bay.

The Fox Bay jetty, with our box being unloaded from the ship

Community Spirit

The sense of community was never more evident than on the arrival of the new mill manager's furniture at the jetty. Practically every able-bodied chap was down there to help unload it.

In the past, this would have been undertaken by the workforce of Packe Brothers, so it was a real testament to the community that everyone pulled together to help this new neighbour.

The two old buildings which the community came together to help transform

Another community event was the clearing out of the old radio building to create a museum of sorts for Falklands War memorabilia. Everyone turned out to help clear rubbish, remove old oil drums, tidy up, and even paint, to help get the building ready.

The cleanup underway, as we remove old oil drums and rubbish

The Islanders were a very resourceful people and they had to be. There was no such thing as plumbers, motor mechanics or electricians out in Camp. If a gutter was blocked, you fixed it yourself. If your Land Rover broke down or your roof was leaking, you fixed it yourself. You get the idea.

Martin & Alissa, played for hours in these packing boxes

Simple delights are at the heart of the Falkland Island life: the satisfaction of hard work; the joy of rest after a long day; delicious food prepared with your own hands; good company, cold beer, and warm friendship.

This was real life, complete with its ups and downs, shared with those who were your friends and neighbours.

Children loved the outdoor life in Fox Bay - Martin has just fallen in a puddle and is covered in mud, yet still smiling

Living in the Falkland Islands is not for the faint hearted. It takes a certain type of person, someone with courage, ingenuity and not afraid of hard work. In return, the rewards of Island life were extensive.

It was a real life, where what you put in determined what you got out. It was a life where people mattered and where a sense of community was valued, needed and appreciated.

CHAPTER 6

The Fox Bay Community

Everyone in Fox Bay had a story, a reason why they had made the journey and chosen to make their home in this remote part of the world. Falkland Islands life was not for the faint-hearted; it attracted those who are ready for adventure, those looking for something different, and those wanting to be part of a close-knit community.

The friends we made and the people we met in the Falkland Islands are some of the warmest, most vibrant, larger-than-life individuals I have ever had the privilege to meet.

Andrew, with Alissa and Martin, in our home with yellow walls

Top among our full-of-life neighbours were Richard and Griz. They overflowed with energy and were brimful of new ideas, typical of the entrepreneurial types who lived in the islands. Richard had worked as the Manager for Packe Brothers in Fox Bay for nearly 20 years. Together with Griz, he pioneered the newly installed wool mill.

Richard & Griz Cockwell were always warm and welcoming. The first time I visited their home, it was an astonishing experience to walk through their long porch which was overflowing with a variety of plants, in stark contrast to the bleaker landscape of the Islands.

Boxing Day barbecue on the beach, with Richard Cockwell

Richard was the organiser, one who carefully thought things through and made sure everything was in place to bring a project to completion. Put simply, he got things done.

Griz was the creative one, the warm "Earth Mother" who made everyone welcome in her home. She was the one who developed creative products for the woollen mill, particularly jumpers and hats which sold like hot cakes to tourists who visited the Islands.

The Cockwells had a lively family of boys: Ben, Adam, and Sam. The youngest, Sam, was a real live wire, around the age of three when we first arrived, so a little older than our son Martin. The older boys were full of zest for life and were at that age where they were eagerly exploring and acquiring knowledge.

Another lively character, John, soon became a good friend. He could turn his hand to pretty much anything, from installing the new drains in Fox Bay to running the Wooden Spoon bar in the old clubhouse as a place for socialising at weekends.

John had a keen sense of humour and the ability to talk the proverbial hind leg off a donkey. It was this that attracted us to enjoy a drink or two at the Wooden Spoon, together with the opportunity to get to meet folk from elsewhere on West Falkland.

John helping us out with the Rayburn
(the Castrol tin has been re-purposed as a peat bucket)

Married to Sue, John had a gorgeous baby girl called Ali (short for Alexandra). John nicknamed himself "the gob", for he had passionate political views, which he did not hesitate to articulate to anyone who would listen. During our time in the islands, John and Sue had a son who they named Joe, which was short for Joseph.

Sue was the perfect foil to John's self-confessed gobbiness - a quiet, determined woman who supported John unequivocally, and reined him in when necessary. We lived next door to John and Sue and they were the best neighbours.

Friendly and unstintingly helpful, John had a gift for making us laugh, in spite of the difficulties which life in Fox Bay brought. His insights were often amusing, including a discussion about why we should only buy flat-packed toilet paper, as we were otherwise paying for shipping on the hole in the middle of the toilet roll!

Austin, leader of the grasslands trial unit in Fox Bay

Austin and Angela lived in the Doctor's House. It was a large property on the far side of the village with sheltered gardens, which one could not help envying. In contrast, our own home in the centre of the village allowed us to be right at the heart of our little community.

West heads and coastline, with penguins on shoreline

Across the road from us lived Nigel and Shirley, who owned and worked the Coast Ridge Farm. Nigel was always to be seen out and about working hard, either zooming by on his quad bike or driving the Land Rover. Shirley, on the other hand, was usually to be found at home or in her beloved polytunnel.

Shirley was a keen gardener, whose green fingers were not limited to the rows of abundant ripening tomatoes. She had coaxed into existence an enviable macrocarpa hedge along the front fence of their home; quite an achievement in an area where salt winds can decimate plant life overnight.

Nigel always gave the impression that there was a lot going on in his mind, but very little was ever expressed verbally. His eyes twinkled when he found something amusing and he worked long hours on the farm.

Shirley was warm-hearted and generous, she often popped across the road, bringing some small treat for our little boy, Martin. It was hard for her when her own boys, Keith and Justin, were away at school in Stanley and she looked forward to the school holidays. She kept busy, filled her time with gardening, decorating and baking, in an attempt to distract herself from missing the boys.

View to Fox Bay Mountain, on West Falkland

Ken and Joyce Halliday played a key role within the community. As Government Agent, Ken held several key roles. He ran the Co-op shop and the Post Office, dealing with eager philatelists from around the world who were keen to get the rare Fox Bay postmark on their First Day Covers.

Ken was also responsible for meeting incoming planes at the landing strip and ensuring that we all received our letters and parcels. Joyce ran the dairy, which supplied the settlement with a plentiful supply of milk and occasionally veal. Their home stood proud at the top of the village green, across from the Post Office and Co-op shop.

Rockhopper penguins, a short drive away from our home

Other neighbours included Martin and Carol, who also had a young family. Unusually, we were there during a time when there were a good number of young children, considering the size of the settlement. We met from time to time to bring all the young children together to play - Austin & Angela's girls, John and Sue's children, Richard and Griz's youngest son Sam, Martin and Carol's son and our son Martin.

Jimmy and Irene were an older couple who became the owners of one of the new houses being constructed in Fox Bay. Everyone in the Falklands had an interesting story to tell, and Jimmy and Irene were no exception. Looking back, I guess Jimmy was probably in his late 40's, but he seemed older to me at the time.

The story we heard was that Jimmy had advertised for a bride and that Irene had responded. She was originally from the Scottish Highlands and Islands and was quiet and reserved with gorgeous deep red hair. In the days where there were no phones, relying only on photographs and letters to choose the right life partner, one can only imagine Irene's thoughts and nerves as she travelled thousands of miles to meet a man she had only encountered on paper. Looking at Jimmy and Irene as they zoomed around on their quad bike, with Irene holding on tightly to Jimmy, it seemed this gamble had paid off wonderfully for them both.

Andrew walking along a typical track in West Falkland

Relatively new arrivals, Alan and Jennifer had arrived from the UK to take over and transform the bunkhouse. Historically, the bunkhouse was somewhere the visiting shearers would stay when coming for the season, remaining empty for much of the year. No longer required for its original purpose, this spacious but externally uninspiring building was to be transformed into a guesthouse. The aim was to create a welcoming place to accommodate the increasing numbers of tourists who were curious to visit the Islands after hearing so much about them during the conflict.

Simon, a young Falkland Islander, had set up a small experimental fishery on West Falkland with the support of the Development Corporation (FIDC). Most days, he was to be seen driving his Land Rover out to tend to his fledgling salmon and mussels. Simon was passionate about this project and utterly committed to seeing it through.

Simon, with his fledgling salmon project

While there were a number of fly-by-night projects set up by FIDC in the wake of the conflict, one had a feeling that Simon would somehow succeed.

Simon typified what was best about the Islanders: their friendliness, "can do" approach and their incredible resilience. Even though he faced numerous challenges, none of them seemed to knock him back for more than a moment. He was usually seen with a serene smile on his face, as if he knew that it was all going to work out just fine, despite how things appeared.

Sunset over Fox Bay

Errol Goss, also an Islander, was a young blonde-haired guy who everyone seemed to warm to. He welcomed us and we spent a few "smokos"' together, talking about life, love and the world. He loved coming over and spending time playing with us and our young son Martin. When he returned to Stanley, we were sad to lose his friendly face from our community.

Su and Rose Binnie lived in an isolated house on the coast ridge about an hour's drive along the track from Fox Bay. Su had lived for more than 40 years in the area, working as a shepherd. Su's real name was Horace, but his little sister was unable to say "you" and called him "Su" and the nickname stuck.

Su loved vehicles and had somehow managed to acquire an eight-wheel amphibious vehicle which he took great pleasure in maintaining, driving around and showing off to curious onlookers.

Although Su and Rose lived some distance from the village, they had been part of the community for many years and were regarded as family. There was a sense of admiration for this retired couple, getting on in years yet living in the middle of nowhere and continuing to battle the elements.

Su & Rosie Binnie's house, view from tussac plantation

Fox Bay West was a settlement immediately opposite us across the bay, not far as the crow flies, but about a 20-minute drive round the track by Land Rover.

Fox Bay West locals included Ron & Sandra Rozee, who had taken over Spring Point with around 5,000 sheep on 25,000 acres; Roy and Chris Bucket who took on Leicester Falls and made exceptionally delicious teaberry buns, and Ian & Marie Gleadell who took on the East Bay section. Many of these folk regularly popped across to the Co-op for their supplies, dropped in at the Wooden Spoon or visited friends on the East shore.

It seemed that folk from every type of background came together to form our small, tight-knit community. We were an unlikely bunch, but our love for this barren landscape drew us together and provided the heart that made Fox Bay come alive.

CHAPTER 7

Island Memories

For me, this lonely spot, this far-off isle, holds many precious memories. In my heart the Islands are England as I dearly wish it could be. Even now, I find my heart yearning for something lost; a time and lifestyle that has come and gone.

The Falklands remind me of times gone by, when neighbours cared about each other, backdoors were left open, and a community worked together to build something greater than themselves.

The wide open, empty spaces of Camp, West Falkland

The Falkland Islanders epitomise what it means to be British. They are genuinely proud to be British, proud of their heritage and confident of their identity. The Falkland Islands feel like a place time forgot, a tight-knit community, living a self-sufficient lifestyle that most can only dream of.

Island life

There was always a feeling of excitement as the FIGAS plane came in to land on the airstrip, knowing that we might soon have post from home. A slow trickle of people wandered across the village green as we stood around awaiting the arrival of the post which, given that there were only about 15 families, did not take long. Ken sorted and collected the post in the little porch of the village store while we waited, chatting together.

The village store was run as a co-operative venture and people would travel in from local settlements to shop there every few weeks. The shop itself was a long low Nissan hut, a half cylindrical building filled with goods that were necessary to life on the Islands such as candles, matches, flour, tinned and dried goods.

With his smiling face, Ken stood behind the counter during the shop's short opening hours. He always went above and beyond the call of duty. If you found yourself in need of an item when the shop was shut and he was in the area, he would open the shop so that you could make a quick purchase. This exemplified the Islanders' mentality of doing what you could to smooth your neighbour's path and make their life easier in some way.

View of Fox Bay village

In my ambition to give myself a purpose and to bring some positive change, I ended up helping to run the West Falkland Co-op. This had really taken off since the closure of the FIC store, when the Fox Bay West store was sold off.

We managed to purchase a few new lines of stock, which were shipped direct from the UK. These included a range of dried goods from Whitworths, which made a welcome change from the canned fruits that were already available.

Ken Halliday had been running the store very capably for many years, but during my time there, we envisaged a larger shop with a wider range of goods available. Suitable Portakabins were purchased from the closing army camp and moved to the village but, in the face of what seemed a mammoth task to prepare them and move all the goods across, the Portakabins remained empty.

On reflection, I daresay I made little difference, apart from annoying dependable Ken. The shop had been working very well until we arrived and probably still is today. I should have remembered and listened to that old adage, "if it ain't broke, don't fix it". Nevertheless, it was fun and kept my mind busy whilst having two small children to look after at home.

As our young son Martin grew, his childhood reflected his surroundings. His first words included "'ot" - as he often reminded me not to touch the "hot" Rayburn. The first animal sound he imitated was the call of a Rockhopper penguin. We thrived on living life outside - fishing, walking and exploring, and Martin seemed to love it too.

Jennifer, holding Martin, on a fishing trip

As Martin grew, the best way of getting around with him was with a pushchair or backpack. My preference was the pushchair, so it was quite normal for me to be seen pushing it across the village green to our hen run, with a bucket of layers meal to feed the hens and collect the eggs in. From there we might go across to check the mail or pop into the shop, if it was open.

On one memorable occasion which is etched into my memory, I walked up to the Halliday's house at the top of the green. I parked Martin and his pushchair by the gate at the end of the house, popping inside for just a few moments.

I was somewhat perturbed on my return, to find a Johnny Rook standing on the ground just a short a few feet away from Martin.

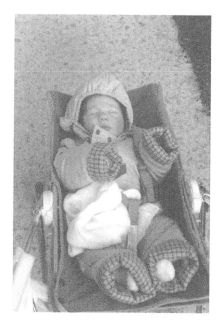

Martin in his pushchair

A Johnny Rook, or striated caracara, is a sizeable bird of prey to be reckoned with, standing around 50 to 60 cm tall. This scavenging Johnny Rook was looking Martin in the eye, but flew off as I walked down the garden path towards him. It was only afterwards that I began to think about what might have happened and made sure never to leave Martin unattended when out in the open air, just in case a hungry Johnny Rook might be watching nearby.

The unusual sight of a gorse hedge

During the war, mines had been laid across the Islands and Fox Bay was no exception. Nearby Weasels Bay and Annie Brook's Bay were mined and therefore out of bounds. Maps of the 'Camp Minefield Situation' were circulated and locals advised to take special care on beaches and rivers, as mines might be washed outside the fenced areas. One of my favourite photos, sadly since lost, was of Andrew proudly holding Martin in front of one of the 'Mines' signs, obscuring the 's', so that it was a picture of him with his son, simply reading 'Mine'.

The joy of real fishing

A favourite pastime for a number of us in Fox Bay was fishing. This was not at all like the recreational fishing we had experienced back in the UK, where one stands for hours not expecting to catch anything and when one does, it is a tiddler, a small fish that one has to throw back.

On the Islands, our fishing had a real purpose. We fished to catch something fresh for supper, for fish to fill the freezer or to share with friends. We fished as a means to bring a change from the delicious but ubiquitous mutton that was an everyday staple.

Jennifer & Andrew fishing at Cheeks' Creek

We had a couple of favourite fishing spots: the nearby Doctors Creek, or along the drive out to Mallard Creek near Su Binnie's place. Sometimes we went alone as a family, or more often with one or two neighbours.

When fishing back in the UK, I had caught a few mackerel out at sea and a pike or two up in Scotland. Nothing prepared me for the delight of fishing for our supper. The location itself was starkly beautiful and peaceful; a wonderful place to stand and contemplate how good life was. The only sound to disturb the peace was an occasional Chinook flying in the distance.

There was great pleasure in picking out the right spinner, casting out and feeling the weight of a fish on your line. Then came the battle to reel it in and land it. Bringing in a mullet weighing several pounds was no mean feat, but the battle and the landing of it was an exhilarating experience.

Andrew, clearly happy to be catching fish for supper

Everything we caught we took home to prepare and freeze down, either in our own freezer or in someone else's. On fishing days we enjoyed freshly caught fish for tea.

There really is nothing like the taste of fresh fish that you had the joy of catching yourself just a few hours earlier.

Most of our fishing trips were for mullet, which were easy to bring in if the tide and conditions were right. Occasionally we went fishing for sea trout, though this required more skill and patience and was not such an easy catch as mullet.

Our neighbour Martin and his son, Jennifer and son Martin,
with their fishing catch of the day

As friends at home did not believe the size of the fish we were catching, we took a memorable photograph of one of the fish, which was almost the same height as Martin. That stopped anybody telling us that we were boasting, as what we told them was no exaggerated "fisherman's tale".

Travels around West Falkland

Trips away from Fox Bay were always an adventure, filled with uncertainty and unexpected challenges. Our first trip up the coast to Port Howard was with just Andrew, myself and Martin.

One never made such a journey without ensuring you had a reliable fully charged CB radio. Although it was only about 50 miles, or around 80 km away, the journey along the track to Port Howard took a full day.

Andrew opening the 'Port Howard' gate,
the first of many on the road north

Depending on the weather conditions, some parts of the track were easier to navigate than others. On one such journey we reached a small farmstead, situated in the middle of nowhere, parked up and were warmly welcomed in for a cup of tea. Our welcome, given that we were strangers to each other, was unexpectedly warm.

Even in this remote corner of the world, hanging on the wall was a framed picture of Her Majesty the Queen, reflecting the pride they felt about being British.

Trips across Camp were not without some risk, as we discovered when crossing one river inlet. The front of the Land

Rover nose-dived into the water, pushing through waves of murky water. Foolhardy and ignorant, we kept going, hoping that the water would not become too deep for our sturdy vehicle.

A typical water crossing with the trusty Landrover

As we motored slowly forward, the nose of the Land Rover created a bow wave and the water came up well above the bottom of the vehicle doors.

Just as I was pondering the wisdom of bringing our young son Martin on the trip, we reached the shallows and drove out safely on the other side. The water sloshed back and forth inside the doors for some weeks to come!

On arrival in Port Howard, we stayed in the bunkhouse and were warmly greeted with excellent food from the bunkhouse chef, whose name I forget but whose welcome I still remember.

Port Howard was still being run as a traditional farm, unlike Fox Bay which had only recently been split into a number of small farm holdings and sold off, after having been run by Packe brothers for many years.

View of Port Howard lodge

This was our first break away from our new home and a welcome change of scene, meeting new faces and hearing their stories.

The bunkhouse at Port Howard

Port Howard from the air

Another memorable experience was driving along the Coast Ridge to Carcass Bay for a family trip to the beach, both for the stunning wild scenery and for the adrenaline rush it gave us.

Andrew & Martin exploring the beach

The Coast Ridge was aptly named as we had to ascend and then descend the ridge in order to reach the beach below. At times like this we appreciated the Land Rover's tenacity and dependability as a trusty workhorse over this wild terrain.

As we ascended at a steep and pretty scary angle, Andrew was anxious that we might not make it, envisaging losing control of the vehicle. Once we reached the top and began descending, it was my turn to feel quite certain that the vehicle would go rolling down the ridge out of control.

Despite our inexperience, the Land Rover proved yet again that it was up to the challenge and we reached the bottom safely. Nonetheless, it was an experience we would not forget in a hurry.

Andrew and Martin on the sandy beach

Carcass Bay was sandy, strewn with dried seaweed and inhabited by clusters of penguins. Martin seemed to be more excited by the seaweed than the penguins, which was understandable for a young lad who in his short life had probably seen more penguins than cars.

Young Martin enjoying the pristine beach

Back home in Fox Bay, the most noticeable thing on the horizon was Fox Bay Mountain, looming on the opposite side of the bay. Every day as we walked around the village collecting eggs, picking up post, or just getting some fresh air, we were often aware of the mountain in the distance. At 1008 feet tall, it was hardly a mountain at all, but it was beautiful to watch its colours change during the seasons. It was at its most magnificent when sprinkled with winter snow, looking just as if someone had dusted it with icing sugar.

Our family back in the UK must have been fed up with seeing photographs of Fox Bay Mountain. We took pictures of it in the snow, in sunshine and on a cloudy day. The mountain intrigued us.

Jen, with Alissa in backpack and Martin standing,
at the top of Fox Bay Mountain (1008')

Finally we were able to make the journey with the 110 Land Rover, taking our young family on a drive up this impressive local landmark. We were able to drive within about 200 metres of the top and walked the final few steps to the summit. It was a proud moment to stand on top of the mountain we had looked at every day for so long, and stare back at our little home across the water in the Fox Bay settlement.

Andrew's role, working with Jim McAdam (from Queen's University in Belfast, Northern Ireland), included the study of tussac grass and exploring how it might help farmers. One of the places tussac grass grows most abundantly is Carcass Island, with its reputation for beauty and wildlife. This provided us with a great excuse for a trip away from Fox Bay to visit the island.

There is always something thrilling about flying over the sea and coming in to land on a small island, and Carcass Island did not disappoint.

Jennifer, Andrew and Martin, amidst the tussac grass

The Islander aircraft landed with a bump and we were greeted in person by Robin and Lorraine McGill, who owned and farmed the island. They drove us to the little house where we were staying for our few days visit.

One of my greatest culinary memories is the delicious bowl of fresh, thick cream which they had so kindly put in the fridge for us. No cream I have ever tasted since compares to the rich deliciousness of that Carcass Island cream, which we enjoyed with local teaberries.

Just a short walk from our little house on the island was an area of coastline teeming with wildlife.

Night herons, known locally as 'quarks', nested in the trees and Magellanic penguins lived in burrows, below ground.

Lone Magellanic penguin in a burrow at Carcass Island

They seemed unafraid of people, so we were able to get really close to them, getting some good photos and creating great family memories.

A night heron, or quark, at Carcass Island

The settlement at Carcass Island

The idyllic views from Carcass Island

Further along the coast, we strolled among the massive hills of tussac grass which stood tall around us. Rounding one corner, we stood stock still as we came face-to-face with a family of elephant seals. Basking on the mud, they were simply enormous, dwarfing young Martin. It was an awe-inspiring sight.

Martin dwarfed by tussac grass

As we got up-close we realised just how massive the seals were. The sounds that emanated from these blubbery mounds were deep-throated bathroom-type noises.

We did not stand around long enough to get too well acquainted, retreating slowly before winding our way back through the tussac grass.

Wherever we travelled across the West, wildlife was abundant and so easy to see close-up. We were often able to get close up to the local wildlife and never once tired of the experience.

Elephant seals on Carcass Island

Elephant seals, close-up view on Carcass Island

Everywhere we went on West Falkland, we received a warm welcome from soon-to-be friends. It was a privilege to be counted as a part of the local community.

Christmas in Camp

Everything about life on West Falkland needed careful planning. There was no such thing as just popping to the local shop to buy a couple of things. Whatever was required had to be anticipated and ordered, often weeks before you needed it.

At that time, the main shopping options were Kays (now Littlewoods) mail order catalogue and the West Store in Port Stanley. Orders to the West Store would usually arrive within a few days, delivered by Islander aircraft. Clothing, homeware and gifts from the Kays catalogue, on the other hand, would take several weeks, but allowed us to access a wider range of goods than were available locally.

Andrew, our Christmas tree and plenty of presents

Planning for Christmas started as early as July, to ensure that everything arrived in plenty of time. A good Christmas dinner took careful planning. Popping to the local supermarket was not an option, so we had to plan ahead to ensure we had all the food needed to put together a delicious feast on the day.

Five-month old Alissa eats the Christmas wrapping paper

Despite missing our family back home in the UK, our first Christmas in Fox Bay was magical. We bought a five-foot artificial Christmas tree from the FIC store, which sat proudly in the corner of our kitchen and was decorated very simply. On Christmas morning there were a good number of gifts waiting to be unwrapped; some bought and wrapped locally, others sent by our UK family and friends.

Family Christmas in Fox Bay

For our first Christmas dinner we enjoyed a gosling, caught by Andrew & John (much to the annoyance of Roy Bucket who had been eyeing it up for his own Christmas dinner!), together with marble-sized potatoes that we had grown ourselves.

Andrew lights our homemade Christmas pudding

The following year we relished eating our own pork, killed earlier that year and saved for the occasion. We served it honey-glazed and it melted in the mouth, all the more delicious for having been raised in our own backyard. There is nothing quite like a home-grown dinner for a truly satisfying meal.

Pride of place on Christmas Day was our homemade Christmas pudding, made with love and given a regular soaking of alcohol (rum or brandy, I don't remember which). The alcohol content ensured a strong and steady flame burned when Andrew lit it on Christmas day.

The flavours of the soaked fruit, together with the alcohol, made for a delicious pudding and, filled with good food, a sleepy afternoon in front of the wood-burning stove. All in all, it was a perfect Christmas.

Sights and Sounds in Camp

Everyone in the Islands listened to Falkland Islands Broadcasting Service (FIBS) on their radio. Patrick Watts' voice was easy to listen to and the radio was a vital lifeline to know what was happening in the world and in Stanley. FIBS would also give updates of news that affected those living on the Islands, particularly items relating to the politics of Britain and the claims made by Argentina.

This really was a local station, so it was no surprise that friends of ours had the occasional spot or show on the radio, including Aiden Kerr, also part of the ARC, and our neighbour Angela, when she was in Stanley. It was comforting to listen to FIBS, knowing that across the Islands others were tuning in too, bringing us closer together.

Views across Camp

My lasting memory of FIBS was the regular request for the annoying song "You're a pink toothbrush, I'm a blue toothbrush", which thankfully I've never heard since leaving the Islands.

Patrick and his team, whilst excellent at sharing international news, knew little of what was going on in our own village in Fox Bay, for that we relied on the RT.

The radiotelephone, or RT, was essential to life in the West. It was used for communications and was vital for spreading news within our community, providing an insight into what was going on in nearby homes.

The RT was strangely comforting, especially when the radio broke in on the quiet of our home, " BKZ, BLW, go down?". To connect with someone, it was essential to know what their call sign was.

The clay patch, several hundred eroded acres,
East Head and Dip Point House in the background

"BKY, BLZ?" was a request to chat. Protocol dictated that once you had responded to someone, the conversation moved down to another channel, in theory for some privacy.

However, it was common knowledge that it would be foolhardy to say anything secret, as there was nothing to stop anyone from turning the radio dial and listening in to your conversation. When the weather outside was not inviting, the RT was far more entertaining than any soap opera.

Whilst most of the conversations were about everyday things, sometimes you got to listen in on some interesting news. People shared their hopes, successes or anxieties, in much the same way as one might today, either by phone or on social media.

On Christmas Day, the radio was unusually silent as each of us celebrated Christmas in our own way. One year, breaking the peaceful silence, came a call. Someone from the bunkhouse was calling a local contractor. Everyone in Fox Bay, both East and West, listened in on that conversation, eager to find out what was so important that it could not possibly wait until after Christmas. It turned out that they were keen to get some pricing for work needed on the bunkhouse, which they were working to transform into a guesthouse. We stopped listening and resumed our family activities, mildly disappointed that it hadn't been a more interesting turn of events.

"Bogged" was the term used when your vehicle became inextricably stuck and needed help and assistance to extract it. More than once we heard a call for assistance from someone who had become "bogged" along the track.

A typical journey across Camp, through water

With no telephones in Camp, the RT was the only real way to communicate, so it was essential to carry it with you on any journey away from the settlement. With no official channel to help you, it was friends and neighbours who would turn up to help get you out.

Pretty much everybody carried in their Land Rover the tools needed to help extract yourself, namely a spade and a "bogging board" comprising of two ex-war Harrier landing mat components, which were light and strong. Sometimes the extraction involved putting something underneath the wheels to help get traction, or using the winch on the front of your vehicle to pull yourself out.

The 110 Land Rover by the peat stacks

However, the best stories came when all else failed and it was necessary to enlist the help of one or more friends. It was pretty humiliating to have to confess to getting bogged. At one time or another, just about everyone suffered the indignity of having to make this call for help. It was great entertainment to listen in on the conversations taking place across the airwaves.

Extracting bogged Land Rovers was comparatively straight-forward to deal with and was a fairly regular occurrence. However, it was with some amusement and considerable trepidation that we heard that the enormous machine brought in to improve the tracks was itself stuck.

Imagine the scene if you will: the pained look on John's face, the quizzical look on Nigel's face, and everyone else putting in their two-penny-worth on how to extract it. The process of extraction took some time and was a complicated affair, involving one of the largest tractors available locally and plenty of onlookers, all happy to generously give their opinion. The machine's misfortune became our amusement and monopolised the topic of conversation for several days.

A helicopter on the green at Fox Bay

Most days, we saw or heard planes or helicopters - either the high-pitched sound of the Islander aircraft in the distance, the deeper sound of a Sea King helicopter, or the distinctive "wokka wokka" sound of an approaching Chinook helicopter.

On one occasion we had the thrilling experience of travelling into Stanley by helicopter (a Wessex or Sea King), because the three FIGAS planes were grounded.

A few days before Christmas there was a visit by Santa, who was choppered in by helicopter and landed on the village green, much to our amusement. This was a side to Santa we had not seen or heard of – clearly he must have left his sleigh in Stanley!

The FIGAS Islander aircraft could carry just a handful of people, no more than 10, but the seats were rarely filled by people as there were usually packets and deliveries to drop off in Camp. A typical flight would involve a number of takeoffs and landings, on the way to your destination. Taking a flight was a great opportunity to meet and chat to people who either lived on, or were visiting, the West.

The tiny landing strips were barely noticeable from the air although some had a small hut or building, as we had at Fox Bay. More often the only thing showing the uninitiated where to land were the waiting Land Rovers and a light strip of grass.

The most memorable landing was on the way out of Stanley one time, when the landing strip was on the beach at Pebble Island, a truly incredible experience. One more thing ticked off the bucket list!

Daily Life in Fox Bay

One of the great things about a small community is that you are likely to meet many of the visitors to the village. Indeed, as there was no hotel or B&B in Fox Bay at that time, sometimes you would also get to host them.

The welcome for visitors to our home was always the same - warm and friendly. Guests would be welcomed into our kitchen as we sat around the Rayburn's warmth enjoying a cup of tea, often with a slice of freshly made bread or cake.

There was only one rule in our home; we did not allow smoking inside the house, partly for health reasons, and partly because smoke made me sneeze! When the Commander of British Forces, known locally as the CBF, visited, he received the same welcome as any guest.

The CBF was, of course, accorded great respect by everyone for his important role on the Islands. We were no exception to this, but rules were rules and we applied them across the board and the CBF was happy to sit smoking on the front step. Our neighbours were pretty horrified, as they took great pleasure in telling us.

Members of the armed forces were at that time stationed in the Falklands for tours of six months or so. They often took their R&R, which stands for "Rest and Recuperation", to spend a few days in Camp. This worked well for everyone. It was great for us to meet and chat with folks from the UK and it was a welcome and refreshing change for them to have a few days enjoying ordinary life away from Mount Pleasant.

If pilots had been out for R&R in the village, they would sometimes come back and do an impromptu fly past - flying low and dipping their wings over the village, as a way of saying thank you to their hosts. One day a Phantom jet flew right down our street, low enough that we could even see the pilot's face. The roaring sound was incredible, deafening us as it passed above our heads. We were astonished to see it flying so low.

Although this courtesy was not uncommon, we heard one story where it backfired. A Phantom fighter pilot showed off a bit too much. He went into a steep vertical climb directly above a house and caused several years of accumulated soot to fall into the house. This may have been an apocryphal tale, but it seemed true enough to us at the time and made us all smile.

One of our favourite visits was by half a dozen members of the Devon and Dorset regiment (now part of The Rifles) visiting our home for R&R. They even found a reason to visit us a second time for an "important" job - picking fresh mussels from the shore at Fox Bay for an important dinner at the Officer's Mess at Mount Pleasant. They loved interacting and playing with Martin, as a number of them were missing their own young children back home.

It was with some amusement that we watched as Martin, nearly three, completed a 100-piece world map jigsaw in a faster time than the soldiers were able to do. Martin loved all this attention and one of my favourite photographs of him was taken with these friendly soldiers, armed to the teeth, in our front yard. Perhaps it was this fond early memory that led him to join the Navy as a medic later in life, going on to serve with the Royal Marines and in Afghanistan.

Visiting soldiers from the Devon and Dorset regiment,
with our son Martin

We had many visitors to our home, mostly soldiers visiting for R&R, but occasionally so-called experts, paid for presumably by the £31 million reparation or rebuilding fund following the conflict.

John had little time for these "experts". It was his contention that these "ex-spurts" were no more than an Ex (has been) and a Spurt (a drip under pressure). In some ways he was right; sometimes it seemed they were people who had finished their career and were now being paid a lot of money to visit and tell us just how we should be doing things.

The size and economy of the Falklands was so different from the UK, as was the lifestyle, so much so that we sometimes wondered how these experts could make a genuinely useful contribution. Not every system that thrives on a large-scale would translate to work well in a small-scale on the Islands.

Andrew wearing his Fjällräven jacket and 'benny' hat,
holding Martin, with penguins in the background

One of these visitors was an expert in developing shops. How he came to be in Fox Bay I have no recollection, but we wondered what he could teach us as a small remote shop with only a handful of families as customers. Our talks with this expert about ways to develop the shop may have moved us forward a few millimetres, but we wondered if it was really worth his consulting fee and the costs for the entire trip.

Other visitors we hosted included Charles Carter, Director of Public Works, and visiting UK MPs including MP George Younger. They were visiting the Falklands to find out more about life there, and met up with locals to find out at first hand what it was that had made Margaret Thatcher feel she was not ready to give them up.

The truth about Falkland Island weather

The Falklands are as far south of the equator as the UK is north. However, there is nothing between the Falkland Islands and the icy landscape of Antarctica, so the winds can sometimes be pretty strong and chilly.

During the war, the Falkland Islands got bad press about the weather, partly because most people in the UK did not realise that as the Falklands are in the southern hemisphere the conflict actually took place in the middle of a Falkland Island winter.

The natural colours of the wool produced by the Falkland Mill

When the wind blew from the south, the Islanders knew to dress accordingly. This was not the time for stylish jackets or good-looking coats; the emphasis was on effectively keeping out the wind. Many locals had "Benny's" - a warm wool hat to keep the warmth in. Before arriving in the Islands we had each invested in Fjällräven jackets which, together with a warm jumper, succeeded in keeping the wind out and the heat in.

We soon procured jumpers knitted with local wool from the Mill in Fox Bay. They were chunky and warm enough to keep out the wind on colder days.

The wool from the Falkland Island Mill came in three natural shades - cream, grey and brown - which local knitters made into various patterns. Knitwear from the Mill was quickly snapped up by the tourist ships that stopped in Stanley.

We sent some of these jumpers home as Christmas presents one year. It is a testimony to the quality of the wool that one of those Falkland jumpers remains one of my father's favourites. Even 30 years later, he still wears it when the weather turns really cold.

The weather in Fox Bay was unpredictable and could change in a moment, as we discovered one Boxing Day. It was December, the middle of a Falkland Islands summer.

All the community had turned out for a midday barbecue, planned because the sun was shining. We drove the short distance out to the edge of the local creek where there was a little bay, just big enough for everyone to congregate and grill some tasty food on the beach.

We stood around under the blue skies enjoying the full hot sun and in danger of getting a little sunburnt. However, by the time we arrived home just a couple of hours later, the sky had turned grey and rain was driving down.

A sunny day for fishing with the family

You could never predict what was going to happen with the weather!

Falkland Islanders were always well-prepared for an unexpected turn of events with the weather, keeping a jumper or coat to hand, even when the forecast was for sunshine.

Green Fingers

Looking enviously across the road at Shirley Knight's vibrant macrocarpa, I was keen to leave my own legacy of our time in Fox Bay. Macrocarpa, a type of cypress, grew low and bushy in the Falklands, ready to brace themselves against a southerly wind.

Shirley had lovingly grown and tended her green fledgling trees with great care, all along the front of the garden. In West Falkland, plants taller than 30 cm were rare, so these were a really unusual sight. To have a hedge or a tree in your garden was something of a major achievement.

View to Stanley harbour, with macrocarpa trees aplenty

With this goal in mind, I ordered some broom and Pinus Silvestris (Scots Pine) seed from the UK, as plants that were most resistant to the salty winds. My aim was to start the seedlings off in the relative safety of the polytunnel, before hardening them off and planting them out.

As planned, they sprouted, grew quickly and thrived, appearing bushy and seemingly hardy in the safety of the polytunnel. One day, filled with buoyant naivety, I planted out the fledgling broom plants on either side of the path leading up to our front door. It was a proud moment.

Sadly that pride was soon dashed by the South Atlantic weather, which I had not fully taken into account. Overnight, the forceful power of a strong wind, which picked up salt from the sea nearby, devastated my fledgling bushes, reducing them to puny leafless sticks and utterly destroying them.

So much for making an impression or leaving a legacy. After this incident, I had a renewed admiration, not only for Shirley, but for anyone who succeeded in battling against nature

The forest on West Falkland - Jennifer dwarfed by the trees

Particularly impressive on West Falkland was the local "forest" and I admired whoever had had the foresight and tenacity to plant it. Driving out to view this phenomenon, it was strange to see this block of dark green trees, standing stark and tall above the bare landscape.

As we drove closer, the height and maturity of the trees was not immediately obvious, but as we parked the Land Rover and walked to the edge of the plantation, we realised that these trees towered several meters above us.

It was an impressive feat indeed, created some years before by an enthusiastic and diligent green-fingered Falkland Islander. What a legacy to leave for future generations!

Martin with his beach combing finds - seaweed!

Visiting Port Stanley

The capital, Port Stanley, is very different in appearance to Camp. It boasted swathes of houses, tarmac roads and prolific plants, even some fully grown trees.

Stanley is situated in a fairly sheltered location and the buildings of the settlement provided an additional element of shelter, creating a micro-climate.

The wide variety of trees, bushes and flowering plants you could see in Stanley were mostly absent from the homes on West Falkland. After spending time on the West, living in a settlement with just 40 or so folk to call our neighbours, visiting Stanley with its 1800 plus population was like visiting another world. To us, this was the "big city".

View from Port Stanley towards Stanley harbour

For us, being in Stanley often meant staying at the home of Fred and Trees, fellow ARC (Agricultural Research Centre) colleagues. Their warm welcome, relaxed atmosphere and Fred's sundowners were legendary. Even today, 30 years later, I have never tasted a gin and tonic like those which Fred took pride in mixing.

Fred loved life in the Falklands, diligently building and setting up his own smoker to smoke locally caught fish. He used his own tied flies to catch sea trout, throwing back anything under ten pounds. Fred's smoked fish was a real treat to enjoy, with its fabulous flavours imparted by the woodsmoke.

Fred Cheong and Simon Hardcastle with their catch

One of our visits to Stanley coincided with the annual Liberation Day Parade, an event where all the Islanders turned out to commemorate the liberation from the Argentine invasion in 1982.

Though it is little spoken of, the events of 1982 indelibly left their mark on every Islander who lived through the experience.

Their horror at being invaded by the Argentinians was eclipsed only by their delight at welcoming the British troops who came to their aid.

The British flag, the Union Jack, flies proudly
during the annual Liberation Day parade

Their gratitude and thanks is honest and heartfelt. While they remain a community that is determined to look forward to the future, the Liberation Day parade is the one day each year when the Islanders permit themselves to look back and remember.

Liberation Day was, and is, a moving occasion.

The day itself was a local Bank Holiday and the whole community turned out for this mid-winter event, which takes place each June.

The day's highlight was a military parade, right along the shoreline on Ross Road. An impressive turnout of a diverse range of military personnel based on the Island paraded along the seafront.

The Annual Liberation Day parade

The road was lined with locals, coming out in the cold to pay their respects and honour those who gave their lives to liberate the Islands. As the British National Anthem began to play, we all joined in singing 'God Save the Queen'.

Finally, a lone bugler paid tribute to the fallen, and tears fell. The memories were fresh and the passion for the Islands was stirred up by the knowledge of how close everyone came to losing their beloved home.

Getting our hands dirty and keeping warm

Pretty much everything in the Falklands was do-it-yourself, from growing your own veg and baking your own bread to the tough job of cutting your own peat. Cutting, drying and bringing in peat is one of the hardest physical jobs for an Islander (excluding sheep-shearing, which was a backbreaking, sweat-dripping task, accompanied by plenty of good-natured joking around).

When we arrived at our little house there was a reasonable stack of good, dry peat waiting for us. However, we knew that if we wanted sufficient peat for the following winter, we would have to cut our own.

Andrew cutting peat and showing his 'Falkland' tan
- from the elbows down and the neck up

Peat was the only heating fuel in the Islands. There was no alternative, so woe betide the man who did not cut sufficient peat to keep his home warm for the winter. Not only would you be exceedingly cold, but you would be derided by your friends and probably be the laughing stock of the West.

You cannot just start cutting peat anywhere. Every home had its own peat bank, so it was essential to cut only from your own bank and not your neighbour's. It was with some trepidation that we drove out to the peat bogs, spade in hand, to make a start.

To cut peat, a good sharp spade was essential, along with strong arm and back muscles, plenty of time and a heck of a lot of patience. The best time of year to start cutting was late spring, which in the Falklands is around October.

The process itself was methodical, involving cutting size-able blocks of soaking wet peat, which cut like butter. Next, the muscles got a good workout as you lifted these hefty blocks up and over the side of the bank, placing them in a pile to dry. The only positive benefit from the incessant wind in the Islands was that it did ensure that your peat dried fairly quickly.

To cut enough peat to keep our home warm for the winter took several trips out to the peat bogs. Each home measured the amount of peat cut in yards, so we proudly recorded that we had cut 23 yards (18th October), then 50 yards (3rd November), 54 yards (29th November) and 91 yards (1st January).

Peat cutting was typically a man's work, though I did cut half a yard myself. The women's role was to help stack and turn the peat, to aid drying in the wind, which I was happy enough to do with our young children looking on.

As the peat gradually dried over the coming months, it turned from chocolate-brownie-smooth and butter-sliceable, to smaller uneven chunks with tiny roots protruding.

Once dried, the peat blocks became so rock hard they could almost be used to hammer in a nail.

In Camp, your peat stack was the measure of your manliness. By the end of the summer, we had enough cut to see us through the winter. Perhaps more importantly, Andrew had proved that he had what it takes to make it in Camp.

Island Life

As part of all the development across the Islands, Fox Bay saw three new homes built. These were known as the Clanwoods - timber-frame homes which arrived in pieces and were put together on-site. The construction and erection of these homes offered considerable entertainment to all of us in Fox Bay.

It seemed strange to us, with homes in the village being mainly one storey high due to the strong winds, that despite the abundance of land, the "powers that be" chose to erect a typical UK-style two-storey home. That seemed to be what the "experts" from London offered, so that was what we got.

One memorable night there was much commotion and the RT radio was alive with talk when the wind blew whilst construction of the homes was still underway. We discovered early the next morning that the first floor of one of the homes had moved several inches from its fixed position. Fixings were hastily put in place so that a repeat of this eventuality could not take place - but it was a source of discussion and amusement for some weeks to come.

The new Clanwood homes being built

On the 27th December 1987, just after Christmas, the first West Falklands Ram and Fleece Show was hosted in Fox Bay. Farmers were invited to display animals in classes, along with the best clip, which was judged by a public ballot. Andrew and Austin ran tours out to the grazing trial plots throughout the day to show visiting farmers the work they had been doing.

It was an unusual sight, seeing over 20 vehicles, mostly Land Rovers, on the green outside the Woolshed and the Wooden

Spoon bar. Our diary records that 40 fleeces, 14 full fleece rams and a dozen clipped rams were shown. It was unprecedented to have more than a hundred people show up, with the Wooden Spoon busy from late morning till well after midnight.

The Ram and Fleece Show was a great social occasion, with a real sense of community as people from far-flung farms came together for the day. Happily, the Show is now an annual event in the Falkland Island calendar.

Jen, crowbar in hand, 'fixing up' a fence,
constructed from repurposed pallets

Clutter, the modern-day ill of many households, is not something that Islanders in Camp were familiar with, as pretty much everything they owned had a purpose.

Anything that did not was quickly repurposed into something useful, or given away to someone who might have a use for it.

Old oil drums became peat bins and pallets became fencing. An Upland Goose wing was the best and only way to sweep away the fine dust from the around the Rayburn. On one occasion, Andrew drove out to take our rubbish to the "tip" and came back having found a cap for our Kenwood liquidiser. Leftover food and vegetable peelings were fed to the pigs or chickens and nothing was wasted.

Martin 'lends a hand' with a crowbar

A testimony to the sense of community was the ease with which people were happy to lend. This might be tools, equipment, or just lending a hand, when needed. There was very little that was superfluous in Falkland Island life – everything had a place, a purpose and a value.

For someone brought up watching the Waltons and Little House on the Prairie on TV, and later The Good Life, with Tom & Barbara, we felt that we were living a self-sufficient life, surrounded by a supportive community, much as they had.

Martin walking along a typical track across Camp,
watched by Andrew

The Islanders have a strong spirit, mixed with humour. They are tough and ready to bounce back, whatever life threw at them. The Islanders are a people I have the utmost admiration and respect for.

There was a sense of community pulling together, especially when life was challenging. The friendships we built there have endured, even across the miles that separate us.

The Falklands are a place and a people that, once encountered, will find their way into your heart and never leave.

CHAPTER 8

Where Are They Now?

A life on the Islands was not for the timid, it required guts and tenacity to make a go of life. Those who lived on the Islands had a wonderful "have a go" mentality, and the Islands repaid them by giving them opportunities to genuinely make an impact.

When it comes to people and personalities, the Falkland Islands had few wallflowers and some delightful larger-than-life characters that we grew to love.

One always had a sense that these were people who were never going to fade into the background, they were going to make their mark, and history has shown this to be true. The people we were fortunate enough to call our friends have indeed gone on to make their own mark on the Islands.

John Birmingham, born in UK, ex-merchant Navy made his mark serving as a member of LegCo (the Legislative Assembly for the Stanley constituency) from 1994 to 2005. He also served on the Legislative Assembly for Stanley from 2008 to 2009. His first wife, Sue, tragically died while the children were still young. John has since remarried and moved to Stanley. Alex still lives and works in Stanley, whilst Joe, her younger brother, has moved to the UK.

Griz Cockwell continues her creative endeavours at Driftwood Studio (driftwood-studio.net), creating evocative and colourful images of her Falkland Island home.

The Cockwell boys - Adam, Ben and Sam, are embracing life in the Falklands. Adam and Sam both live and work in Stanley, whilst Ben lives in Fox Bay.

Richard Cockwell, has put his management experience with Packe brothers to good use, serving on the Legislative Council for Camp from 1997 to 2009. In 2012, Richard travelled to Buckingham Palace to receive an OBE from the Queen for his work in promoting the Falklands internationally.

Shirley and Nigel Knight remained at Coast Ridge Farm. When Margaret Thatcher visited Fox Bay, Shirley character-istically made a brave but emotional speech. As Shirley spoke about those whose lives have been lost fighting for freedom, she was overcome with emotion. Mrs Thatcher came over and hugged her, mother to mother, a poignant moment. Shirley died suddenly in 2010, but Nigel is still to be seen about with that wry smile and a twinkle in his eye.

Ken & Joyce Halliday have moved into Stanley. Ken has given up his role as Postmaster and their old home in Fox Bay now houses the Post Office Museum.

Errol Goss is back in the Islands after spending several years away.

Su & Rose Binnie continued to live on the Coast Ridge until Rose had a fall, at which point they moved into Fox Bay to be less isolated. Rose died in 1995 but Su continued to live in Camp, no doubt zooming around on his quad bike until his death at the age of 92, in 2008.

Andrew & Jennifer Carter's time in the Falklands came to an end when the Overseas Development Administration (ODA) handed over the Agricultural Research Centre (ARC) to the Falkland Islands Government in June 1988, and Andrew's contract ended.

Jen, with hands in pockets to keep warm,
at our favourite fishing spot at Fox Bay

Each day in Fox Bay was an adventure. Our lives now reflect a thirst for wild spaces and encounters with nature.

The Falkland Islands population, has swelled to over 2500 at the time of writing. The issue of sovereignty continues to be heatedly discussed. The promise of oil wealth continues, while the Islands' economy continues to develop and grow.

We fell in love with the Islands and her people. I have never lived anywhere where one felt so proud to be British. It is my hope the Islands will remain under British sovereignty.

This book is a tribute to the Islanders themselves, a strong people, proud to call themselves British, proud of the life they have carved out for themselves on the Islands, and strong enough to withstand whatever changes they may have to face in the coming years.

Postscript

Life in Camp has changed significantly since the mid-1980s.

RT is no longer essential to communications. Broadband and mobile phone coverage extend throughout West Falkland. FIBS are still broadcasting and keeping the community informed and together.

The tracks on West Falkland have been upgraded to all-weather tracks, so the 82km trip to Port Howard that once took the best part of a day can now be completed in around an hour and a half. The tracks are now passable year-round, not just in summer. A regular ferry service now links East and West Falkland, carrying cars, passengers and cargo.

The population has boomed, from 1,849 in 1980, just before the war, to 2,932 in 2012, an increase in population of more than 50%.

Tourism is a growth industry, with over 40,000 cruise passengers (as at 2015) and 8,000 tourists visiting each year (as at 2012).

The harsh, bare beauty of the Islands remains the same as it has always been. The welcome in the Islands will still be a warm one.

Life in Camp still requires the same courageous, hardy spirit that it always has. Perhaps one day I will return, but until then I dream of stark landscapes, roast mutton and a people who warmed my heart and welcomed me into their homes.

If you visit the Islands, I trust that your welcome will be warm and that you will grow to love their untouched wild beauty. Please enjoy a smoko for me!

Acknowledgments

With grateful thanks to Andrew Carter for his contributions, without which this book would not have been possible.

With thanks to our friends in the Islands, especially John, Griz, Richard, Errol and Simon for your support and friendship.

About the Author

Jen Carter is a mother to three grown up children and a grandmother. She enjoys countryside walks with her cocker spaniel and lives in Wiltshire, not too far from the World Heritage Site of Stonehenge.

Any mistakes in this book are entirely her own and partly due to the passage of time and an imperfect memory.

You can let Jen know of any factual errors by messaging her Facebook author page, www.facebook.com/JenniferCarterWriter.

The photos included in this book were taken about 30 years ago, so are of far poorer quality than even the average smartphone might take nowadays. Nevertheless, they are included to record and illustrate some of everyday Falkland Life as it was back then.

If you've enjoyed reading this, it would mean so much to Jen if you could leave a review on Amazon. Thank you.

Also by Jen Carter

Women of Courage - tells the remarkable untold stories, challenges & triumphs of thirty-one ordinary, yet extraordinary, Bible women.

Daily Readings for Difficult Days - a daily devotional for Christian women going through difficult times, including divorce, death of a loved one, depression and other struggles.

A Christmas Surprise - a children's story, telling the real Christmas story, told by those who saw it.

Powerful Positive Affirmations - find encouragement in these words from the heart of God the Father.

These books are also available as audiobooks.

Made in the USA
Coppell, TX
29 December 2022

10065252R00079